Story Central

Student Book **1**

GW00691271

Viv Lambert
Mo Choy

macmillan
education

Contents

Chapter	Grammar	Vocabulary	Story	CLIL	Song and Phonics
7 **Strange Creatures** *page 68*	It has four legs. It doesn't have any arms. She has two eyes. How many legs does she have? She doesn't have any legs.	Body parts Adjectives	**Good Friends**	*Science*: planets and space	*I'm an Alien* long **a**
8 **I Like Food!** *page 78*	I like pizza, but I don't like broccoli. Do you like pizza? Yes, I do. / No, I don't.	Food Days of the week	**I Like Cake!**	*Home economics*: healthy and unhealthy foods	*Ice Cream and Cake* short **i** and long **e**
9 **Sports and Music** *page 88*	He can run. He can't skate. Can she sing? Yes, she can. / No, she can't. Can you ride a bike? Yes I can / No I can't.	Sports Musical instruments	**The Magic Violin**	*Social sciences*: instruments around the world	*Let's Play Together* short **a** and short **u**
Grammar Reference *page 98*	Chapters 1–9 Grammar Review and Sentence Makers				

Competencies

me	act	think	learn	communicate
Activities that encourage children to accept responsibility and reflect on the consequences of lifestyle choices.	Activities that develop societal understanding and identification of children's own circumstances in a wider context.	Activities that develop critical thinking skills to reflect upon, manipulate, process, and interpret information.	Activities that foster learner autonomy, and allow children to demonstrate and put into practice learning strategies.	Activities that promote interpersonal and collaborative skills, develop teamwork, and allow children to express opinions and ideas.

Story Central

1))) **Listen and sing.**

Welcome, Welcome

Welcome, welcome, everyone!
Story Central is a lot of fun.

Please come in and close the door.
Sit on a chair, sit on the floor.

Welcome, welcome, everyone!
Story Central is a lot of fun.

Walk around and take a look.
Watch a show, choose a book.

Welcome, welcome, everyone!
Story Central is a lot of fun.

Read a poem, play a game.
Listen to a story, come again!

Welcome to Story Central

1))) Listen and read. Then act out.

2))) Listen and point. Then complete the blanks.

1	one
2	two
3	-----
4	four
5	five
6	six
7	-----
8	eight
9	nine
10	-----

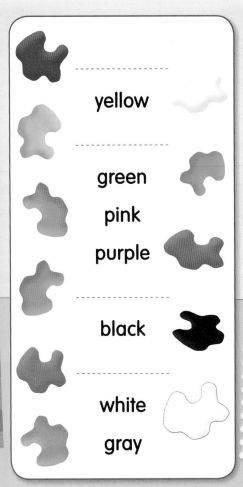

yellow

green

pink

purple

black

white

gray

abc -----

efghij -----

lmno -----

qrst -----

vwxyz

3 Write about you.

Name: -------------------------------------

Age: -----------------------------------

Grade: ---------------------------------

Teacher: -------------------------------

Favorite color: -------------------------

Favorite number: -----------------------

Favorite story: -------------------------

Listen and number. Then say.

1))) **Complete the pictures. Then listen and number.**

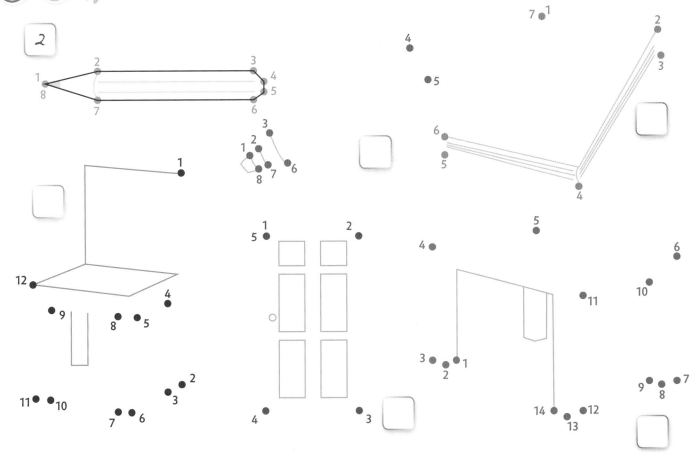

2 **Point to the pictures. Ask and answer.**

What is it?

It's a pencil.

3))) **Listen. Then play a guessing game.**

Is it a chair?

No, it isn't.

Is it a table?

Yes, it is.

Grammar Central

What is it? It's a pen.
Is it a pencil?
Yes, it is. / No, it isn't.

1)) **Listen and read. Then act out.**

Hello, Ellie. How are you?

I'm fine, thank you. How are you, Libby?

I'm fine, too, thanks.

Look! It's a magic pen …

Chen's Magic Pen

1

What is it?

It's a tree.

3

I'm King Jade. What's your name?

My name's Chen.

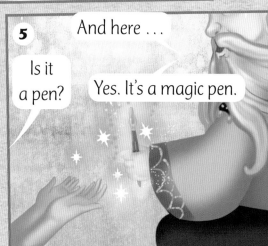

5

And here …

Is it a pen?

Yes. It's a magic pen.

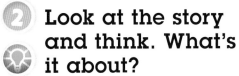

2 Look at the story and think. What's it about?

3))) **Listen and read. What items are in the story?**

a pen ☐

a table ☐

a chair ☐

a book ☐

a pencil ☐

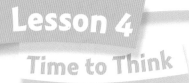

1. Read the story in your Reader.

I Can Read!
What's on the cover?

Chen's Magic Pen
书
Ruth Stitt

2. Check (✔) the items that Chen draws.

3. What would you ask Chen to draw?

4. Talk about the story.

Do you like the story?

  Listen and match. Then sing.

Thank You, Chen

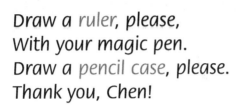

SCHOOL

Draw a bag, please,
With your magic pen.
Draw a crayon, please.
Thank you, Chen!

Draw a ruler, please,
With your magic pen.
Draw a pencil case, please.
Thank you, Chen!

Draw a notebook, please,
With your magic pen.
Draw an eraser, please.
Thank you, Chen!

2 **Play a guessing game.**

Is it an eraser?

Yes, it is.

3 **Listen and say the chant.**

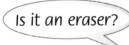

Pen and pencil, pencil and pen.
Pink pencil, purple pen.

1))) **Listen and read.**

Welcome to Story Central

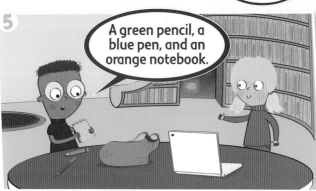

2 **Answer the questions.**

1 What color is the pen? ....It's blue....
2 What color is the notebook? ....
3 What's this?

.... an eraser.

.... a pencil.

Grammar Central

What color is it?
It's green.
A blue pen. / An
orange notebook.
It isn't a ruler.

1))) **Listen and read. Write the missing words.**

What is a Tree?

It's an apple.

It's my home.

It's a pencil.

It's a _____,

It's a _____,

2 **Draw one more item on the tree.**

3 **Look at the tree. Ask and answer.**

What is it?

It's a notebook.

What color is it?

It's red.

4 **Class Vote!**

Grow more trees. Yes or no?

Find Out More!

Why are trees important? Search the Internet or ask your teacher.

Project

Prepare

1 Make a magic picture.

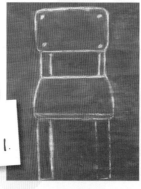

It's a chair.
By Mia Coles. Grade 1.

Showcase

2 Tell the story. Use your magic pictures.

It's a horse. An orange horse.

Thank you, Chen!

1 **Match the questions and answers.**

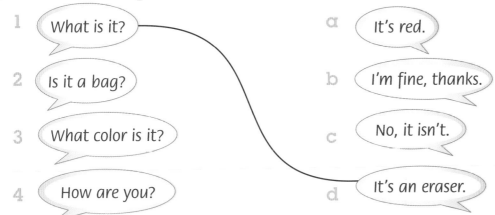

1 What is it?

2 Is it a bag?

3 What color is it?

4 How are you?

a It's red.

b I'm fine, thanks.

c No, it isn't.

d It's an eraser.

2))) **Listen and circle. Then write.**

1 a red ruler

2

3

4

5

6

3 **Think about Chapter 1. Color the books.**

GREAT!

OK.

I'M NOT SURE.

Treasure Hunt!

Look back at pages 4 and 5. Find:

a purple notebook

Chapter 2

My Toys

Lesson 1

1)) **Listen and write the letter. Then say.**

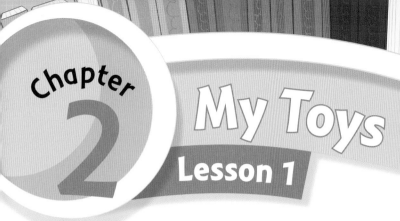

TOYS

a a car	**b** a robot	**c** a ball
d a doll	**e** a bike	**f** a teddy bear

My Birthday List

a robot   b

a doll

a teddy bear

a car

a bike

a ball

1))) **Listen and point.**

2))) **Listen again and circle. Then check with a friend.**

1 This is / That's my ball.

2 This is / That's my car.

3 This is / That's my robot.

4 This is / That's my teddy bear.

3))) **Listen. Then ask and answer.**

Grammar Central

This is **my** doll.
That's my bike.
Is **this your** bike?
Is **that your** doll?

1 Listen and read. Then act out.

Hello, Ellie. Is this your ball?

Yes, it is.

What's your favorite toy?

My teddy bear. It's small and yellow.

The Princess and

4 My teddy bear is my favorite toy!

Oh, Polly! How old are you?

I'm 13.

6 Look at this teddy bear.

That isn't my teddy bear. My teddy bear is small.

8 Please help Princess Polly. Find my teddy bear. It's small and yellow.

the Teddy Bear

5 Here's a teddy bear.

That isn't my teddy bear. My teddy bear is yellow.

7 Please help...

9 Please help Princess Polly. Find my teddy bear. It's small and yellow.

Oh! This teddy bear is small and yellow!

2 Look at the story and think. What's it about?

3))) Listen and read. What toy is in the story?

a teddy bear

a bike

a car

1))) Read the story in your Reader.

I Can Read!
What's the story title?

2 Check (✔) Princess Polly's teddy bear.

3 Draw something to give to Daisy.

4 Talk about the story.

Do you know another story about a princess?

Lesson 5

Song

 1)) **Listen and point. Then sing and shout your name.**

December   January

November

When's Your Birthday?

February

January, February,
March, April, May.
June, July, August.
When's your birthday?

September, October,
Let's play a game.
November, December,
Shout out your name!

October

March

September

April

August

May

July   June

When's your birthday?

2 **Class survey. Ask and answer.**

When's your birthday?

It's in December.

 **3**)) **Listen and say the chant.**

June, July, or January?
January, July, or June?
When's your birthday?
Is it soon?

January	February	March	April
May	June	July	August
September	October	November	December

Lesson 6

1))) **Listen and read.**

Happy Birthday, Tom!

When's your birthday, Biblio?

It's in January.

Ping!

BIRTHDAY REMINDER: TOM!

What's that?

When's his birthday?

It's in April. Today!

Oh, wow! How old is he?

He's seven.

What's that?

It's a card for Tom. His favorite toy is a robot.

Dear Tom,
It's April.
You're seven today
Happy Birthday!

Happy Birthday, Tom!

Surprise!

Thank you.

2 **Complete the blanks for Tom.**

1 When's .... *his* .... birthday?
   It's in ....

2 How old is .... ?
   He's ....

Grammar Central

When's **his** birthday?
It's in April.
How old is he?
He's seven.

1 **Look and find shapes around you.**

Shapes and Numbers

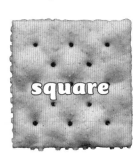 square

 circle

 rectangle

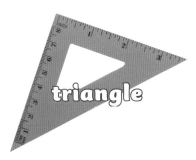 triangle

2)) **Listen and match. Then say.**

thirteen　　eleven　　**fifteen**　　**eighteen**　　seventeen

11 **12** **13** **14** **15** **16** **17** **18** **19** **20**

fourteen　　**twelve**　　twenty　　**sixteen**　　nineteen

3 **Look at the doll. Count and write.**

 15

4 **Class Vote!**

Math is fun! Yes or no?

Find Out More!

What other shapes are there? Search the Internet or ask your teacher.

Prepare

1 Make a toy poster.

My Favorite Toy

This is my teddy bear.
It's blue.

Showcase

2 Tell the story. Use your posters.

Look at this teddy bear.

That isn't my teddy bear.

1)) **Listen and check (✔) (Yes, it is.) or cross (✗) (No, it isn't.).**

2 **Look at the pictures. Complete the sentences.**

MARCH

1 She's 7. Her favorite toy is a teddy bear. Her name is ....

2 .... 17. ....
birthday is in March. Her favorite
toy is a robot. ....
name is Libby.

3 **Think about Chapter 2. Color the books.**

GREAT!

OK.

I'M NOT SURE.

Treasure Hunt!

Look back at pages
4 and 5. Find:

a ball

Chapter 3

Wild Animals

Lesson 1

1))) **Listen and number. Then say.**

1 a giraffe   4 a monkey
2 an elephant   5 a lion
3 a crocodile   6 a tiger

1 🔊 **Listen and point. Then say.**

2 🔊 **Listen and circle.**

1 What are these?

They're tigers / (monkeys).

2 What are those?

They're giraffes / elephants.

3 What are these?

They're monkeys / lions.

4 What are those?

They're crocodiles / elephants.

3 **Now check with a friend.**

What are these?

They're monkeys.

Grammar Central

What are these?
They're tigers.
What are those?
They're elephants.

Lesson 3

Tell Me a Story

1 Listen and read. Then act out.

Let's look at these books about toys.

OK.

No. Let's look at those books about animals.

The Hungry Giraffe

1

2

An elephant! Please help. Those leaves are green, but the trees are tall.

4

What are these?

They're bananas.

No, thank you!

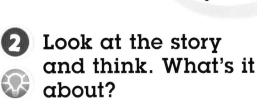

2 Look at the story and think. What's it about?

3))) Listen and read. What animals are in the story?

a giraffe

an elephant

a crocodile

Lesson 4

Time to Think

1))) Read the story in your Reader.

2 Number the pictures in order.

3 Which friends do you share with?

I share with _____.

4 Talk about the story.

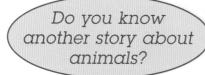

Do you know another story about animals?

1))) **Listen and point.**
   Then sing.

Happy Giraffe

Look at those scary tigers!
They're orange, black, and white.
They're very scary tigers.
And they're hungry tonight.

Look at these snappy crocodiles!
They're long and they're green.
They're snappy, snappy crocodiles.
With big scary teeth!

I'm a happy giraffe.
I'm thin and I'm tall.
I love these green leaves.
I'm not hungry at all.

2 **Play a guessing game.**

tall   long   thin   scary   hungry

They're long
and green.

They're
crocodiles!

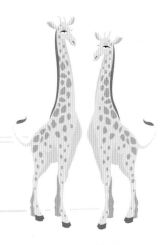

3))) **Listen and say the chant.**

We're tall. We're thin. We're tall
and thin. Two giraffes are tall and thin.

Lesson 6

(1)))) **Listen and read.**

A Scary Animal!

1

Help! A scary animal!

No, it isn't.

Wow! Is it a crocodile?

2

A monkey? Are monkeys scary?

No, they aren't.

3

Is it orange, black, and white?

No, it isn't a tiger.

4

Aha! Is it small and black?

Yes, it is. It's a scary spider!

5

Aww. Spiders aren't scary.

Yes, they are!

No, they aren't. They're cute! Look!

(2) **Write Tom's answers.**

1 Is it a crocodile? No, it ...._isn't_............ .

2 Is it a spider? ....

3 Are monkeys scary? ....

4 Are spiders scary? ....

Grammar Central

Spiders **aren't** scary.
Are monkeys scary?
Yes, **they are**. /
No, **they aren't**.

1))) Listen and read.

Hungry Animals

Look at these **giraffes**. They're tall. They eat leaves from these tall trees.

These animals are **zebras**! They aren't tall. They eat grass. **Elephants** eat grass and leaves, too.

What's this? It's a **leopard**. Leopards eat meat. **Lions** eat meat, too. Watch out, zebras! Those lions are scary. They eat zebras and other animals.

Some animals eat meat and some animals eat grass, fruit, and leaves. **Monkeys** eat meat and fruit. What do you eat?

2 Write the animals in the correct places.

lions

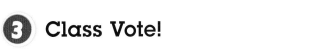

3 Class Vote!

Leopards are scary. Yes or no?

Find Out More!

Choose an animal. Find out what it eats. Search the Internet or ask your teacher.

Project

Prepare

1 Choose a mask to make.

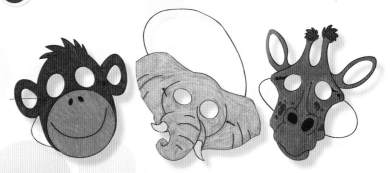

Showcase

2 Tell the story. Use your masks.

What are these?

They're bananas.

1 Look and complete the blanks.

1 What are these? They're ......elephants.......

2 What ....? .... lions.

3 What are those? They're ....

4 .... are those? .... tigers.

2 Circle the correct answer.

1 Are crocodiles long and green? Yes, they are. / No, they aren't.

2 Are lions scary? Yes, they are. / Yes, it is.

3 Are giraffes small? Yes, they are. / No, they aren't.

4 Are spiders tall? No, it isn't. / No, they aren't.

3 Think about Chapter 3. Color the books.

GREAT!

OK.

I'M NOT SURE.

Treasure Hunt!

Look back at pages 4 and 5. Find:

two scary lions

My House
Lesson 1

1)) Listen and number. Then say.

bedroom

bathroom

garage

| living room

kitchen

yard

1 2 3 4 5 6

1))) **Listen and number. Then say.**

in the bag [1]

under the table [ ]

behind the door [ ]

on the chair [ ]

2))) **Now look again. Where's the mouse?**
Listen and (circle) the correct answer.

1 It's (behind) / in the bag.

2 It's on / under the chair.

3 It's under / on the table.

4 It's on / behind the cat.

3 **Ask and answer.**

Where's the mouse?

It's in the bedroom. It's under the chair.

Grammar Central

Where's the cat?
It's **in** the living room.
It's **behind** the door.

Chapter 4

39

Lesson 3

Tell Me a Story

1)) Listen and read. Then act out.

2 Look at the story and think. What's it about?

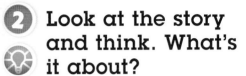

3))) Listen and read. What rooms are in the story?

kitchen

bathroom

living room

1))) Read the story in your Reader.

I Can Read!

When do we use these?

2 Number the rooms in order.

3 Draw something valuable.

4 Talk about the story.

Do you like mystery stories?

1 🔊 **Listen and find the shoe. Then sing.**

Song

One Shoe is Missing

One shoe is missing.
It's a mystery.
One shoe is missing.
Help me find it, please!

It isn't in the bedroom,
Under the bed.
It isn't in the closet,
Or under the desk.

It isn't in the kitchen.
It isn't on the floor.
It isn't in the garage,
On the shelf behind the door.

It isn't in the living room,
Behind the TV,
Or under the sofa.
Help me find it, please!

2 **Ask and answer.**

Where's the ball?

It's under the bed.

3 🔊 **Listen and say the chant.**

A ruler, a ruler. A long, red ruler.
A long, red ruler in the living room.

Lesson 6

1))) **Listen and read.**

Mystery Day

Hello. Welcome to our mystery day. Ask Biblio for a clue.

Stand up tall. What can you see? It's red and white. It begins with B!

B is for … book! Look on the shelf, Tom.

A red and white book… It's on the shelf!

Open the book.

It's a clue!

Go to the sofa. Don't sit down. Find your prize. Eat it now!

The sofa, quick!

Don't sit down!

A cake. Eeeew!

2 **Look at the story.**
Circle the correct words.

1 Stand up / Don't stand up tall.

2 What can you see?

3 Sit down / Don't sit down on the sofa.

4 The prize begins with b / c / e.

Grammar Central

Stand up.
Don't sit down.
Open the book.

1))) **Listen and read.**

Different Homes

What is a home? Where you live is your home. Do you live in a house or an apartment? Look at this boat. It's a home, too. It's a houseboat!

Take a look. The kitchen is in the living room. The bedroom is in the living room, too. At night, the sofa is a bed. Where's the TV? It's on the shelf. Is that a closet? No, it's a bathroom.

2 (Circle) **T (true) or F (false).**

1 The bedroom is in the living room. (T) / F
2 The sofa is a bed. T / F
3 The TV is on the shelf. T / F
4 The TV is under the desk. T / F
5 The bathroom is in the kitchen. T / F
6 The kitchen is in the closet. T / F

3 Class Vote!

House or houseboat?

Find Out More!
Find more unusual houses. Search the Internet or ask your teacher.

Prepare

1 Make a mystery house.

1

2

3

Showcase

2 Tell the story. Use your mystery house.

Hmm, is it under the table?

1)) **Listen and draw lines. Then write.**

1 The doll is .... on .... the bed.
2 The bag is ....,
3 The cat is ....,
4 The car is ....,

2 **Choose the correct instruction. Then write.**

Come in.   Don't sit down.   Open the door.

....

3 **Think about Chapter 4. Color the books.**

GREAT!
OK.
I'M NOT SURE.

Treasure Hunt!

Look back at pages 4 and 5. Find:

a desk

1)) Listen and number. Then say.

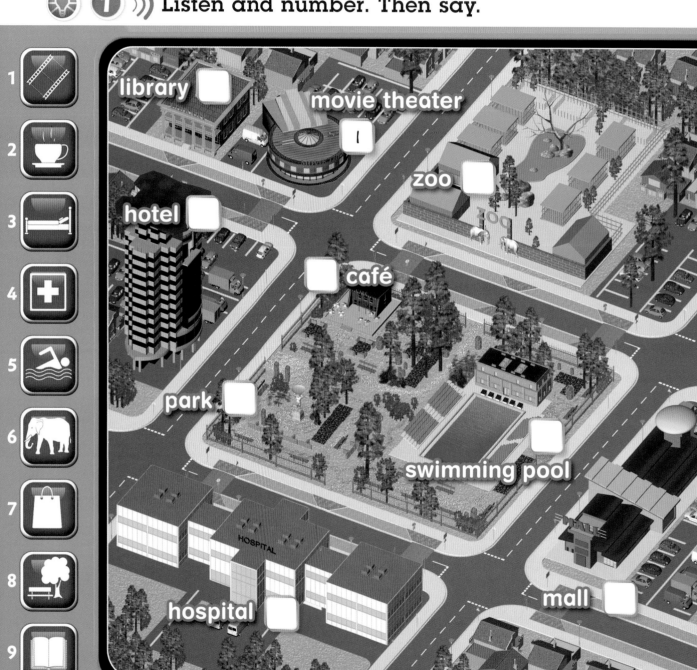

library

movie theater
1

zoo

hotel

café

park

swimming pool

hospital

mall

1
2
3
4
5
6
7
8
9

1 **Look, count, and write.**

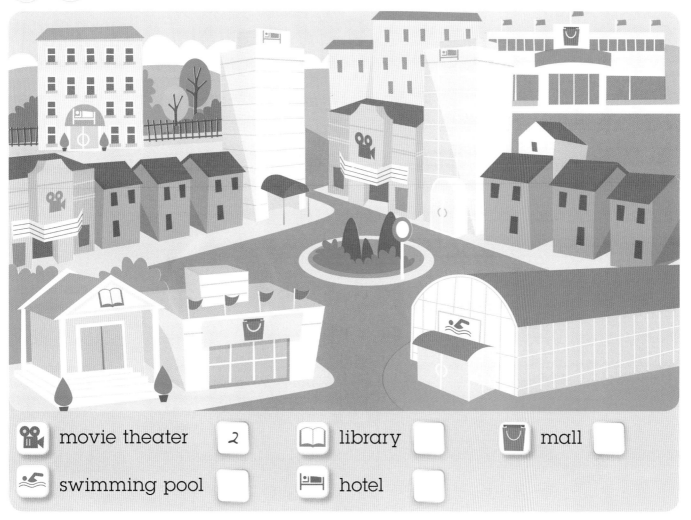

 movie theater `2`   📖 library ☐   🛍 mall ☐

🏊 swimming pool ☐   🛏 hotel ☐

2 🔊 **Listen and (circle) T (true) or F (false).**

1 There's a library.   Ⓣ/ F   3 There isn't a swimming pool.   T / F

2 There are three malls. T / F   4 There are two movie theaters. T / F

3 **Ask and answer.**

Is there a zoo?

No, there isn't.

How many hotels are there?

There are three.

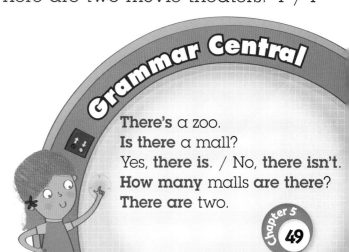

Grammar Central

There's a zoo.
Is there a mall?
Yes, **there is**. / No, **there isn't**.
How many malls **are there**?
There are two.

Lesson 3

Tell Me a Story

1))) **Listen and read. Then act out.**

Excuse me, where are the comics?

They're across from the computers, next to the books.

Thanks!

CAPTAIN NAVIGAT

Come on, Sniffer the Superdog! Let's go!

Oh, no! It's Maria's birthday today. Is there a mall near here?

There's a mall across from the movie theater on Second Avenue.

Help! Please help! Is there a hospital in this town?

There's a hospital on First Avenue. Come with us.

nk
u!

Thanks, Captain Navigate!

2 Look at the story and think. What's it about?

3))) Listen and read. What places are in the story?

a mall

a movie theater

a hospital

a zoo

1.)) Read the story in your Reader.

I Can Read!
What are these?

ZOOM
WHOOSH!

2. Who is good? Who is bad? Write G (good) or B (bad).

3. Write. Ask Captain Navigate for help.

4. Talk about the story.

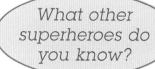

What other superheroes do you know?

Listen, count, and write. Then sing.

Beep, Beep, Beep!

There are cars and buses on the street.

Zoom! Vroom! Beep! Beep! Beep!

How many cars are there on the street? ☐

How many buses? Zoom! Vroom! Beep! ☐

There are trucks and taxis on the street.

Zoom! Vroom! Beep! Beep! Beep!

How many trucks are there on the street? ☐

How many taxis? Zoom! Vroom! Beep! ☐

There are vans and motorcycles on the street.

Zoom! Vroom! Beep! Beep! Beep!

How many vans are there on the street? ☐

How many motorcycles? Zoom! Vroom! Beep! ☐

② Ask and answer.

How many buses are there?

There are two.

③ Listen and say the chant.

The bus goes beep, the van goes vroom.
Beep, beep, vroom, beep, beep, vroom.

Lesson 6

1)) Listen and read.

The Superheroes' Party

1 Look! There's a superheroes' party at the café in Green Park today.

Cool!

2 Is there a bus to the park?

No, there isn't, but there are a lot of taxis. Taxi!

3 Green Park, please.

Where's Green Park?

It's across from the mall, next to the zoo.

4 Take the second left. Go straight. Then take the first right.

5 Here we are at Green Park, but where's the café?

Look! It's Captain Navigate. Let's follow him!

6 Look, the Green Park café! How many superheroes are there?

This is fun!

2 Look at the story. Complete Libby's directions to Green Park.

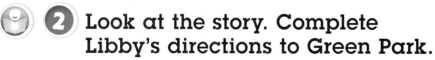

1 Where's Green Park?

2 It's .... next to .... the zoo.

3 Take the ....

4 Go ....

5 Then, take the ....

Grammar Central

Take the first left.
Go straight.
It's **across from** the mall.

1))) **Listen and read. Then write the number of the correct picture.**

TRANSPORTATION

Bangkok is a big city in Thailand. There are a lot of houses, malls, and cafés. The streets in Bangkok are very busy. There are cars and motorcycles. There are buses and taxis. ☐ There are tuk-tuks, too. Tuk-tuks are blue and red. ☐

There's a long river in Bangkok called the Chao Phraya River. There are river buses ☐ on the Chao Phraya River.

2 **Check (✔) the transportation in your town. Then talk to a friend.**

> In my town, there are buses and taxis.

taxis ☐ tuk-tuks ☐ river buses ☐ buses ☐

3 **Class Vote!**

Tuk-tuk or river bus?

Find Out More!
**What other transportation is there?
Search the Internet or ask your teacher.**

Project

Prepare

1 Make a town map and badges.

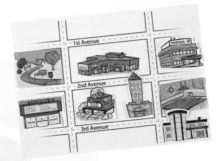

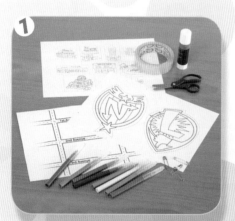

Showcase

2 Tell the story. Use your town map and badges.

There's a mall across from the movie theater on Second Avenue.

Thanks, Captain Navigate!

1))) **Listen and write the numbers. Then answer.**

library [1]   mall [ ]   hospital [ ]
hotel [ ]   café [ ]   park [ ]

WELCOME TO Little Town

1 Is there a hospital? ....

2 Is there a zoo? ....

3 Is there a hotel? Yes, there are ....

4 How many cafés are there? ....

2 **Look at the map. Complete the directions from the café to the swimming pool.**

Go straight.
Take the ....
Then take the ....
It's ....
the bathroom.

3 **Think about Chapter 5. Color the books.**

GREAT!
OK.
I'M NOT SURE.

Treasure Hunt!

Look back at pages 4 and 5. Find:

a red bus

Chapter 6

My Family
Lesson 1

1))) Listen and number. Then say.

mom [1]   grandma [ ]   brother [ ]   aunt [ ]

grandpa [ ]   uncle [ ]   dad [ ]   sister [ ]

1)) **Listen and read. Then check (✔) the correct picture.**

I have a mom and a dad.	My grandpa is tall.
I don't have a brother.	I have two grandmas.
I have two sisters.	I don't have any aunts or uncles.

2 **Look at the other picture. Complete the sentences.**

My mom is tall.

I have _____ brothers.

I _____ have a grandpa.

I _____ a grandma.

3 **Talk to a friend about your family.**

I have three sisters and one brother.

Grammar Central

I have two sisters.
I don't have a brother.
I don't have any brothers or sisters.

Tell Me a Story

1 🔊 Listen and read. Then act out.

Hello, Tom. Who's this?

Hi, Libby. This is my little brother, Bobby.

Hi, Bobby. Nice to meet you!

Hello, Libby.

Here's a story for you.

1 I'm Nadia. I have a big family. I have a little sister, Olga.

2 I'm hungry!

I don't have any food, Olga. Sorry.

4 This is my brother Yuri. I have three brothers.

Can I help you, Dad?

Yes, please. The turnip is very big.

The Giant Turnip

3

It's OK, Olga. Look! The turnip is big now. Let's eat it!

That's my dad.

5

This turnip is very big.

Where are your brothers? Sergei! Mikhail! Come here!

2 Look at the story and think. What's it about?

3))) Listen and read. Who is in the story?

dad ☐

sister ☐

uncle ☐

1)) Read the story in your Reader.

I Can Read!
Look at picture 13 in your Reader. Why is 'HOORAY!' in capitals?

2 Complete the blanks.

I have .... brothers.
I have .... sister.

3 Who helps you? Say thank you.

THANK YOU

To ....

Thank you for ☐ my present.

☐ helping me with my homework.

☐ being my friend.

From ....

4 Talk about the story.

Do you know any stories about families?

Song

1))) **Listen and number. Then sing.**

My Pets

I have a turtle [2] and a cat. [ ]
I have a hamster [ ] and a rat. [ ]
I have a fish [ ] and a mouse. [ ]
They all live here in my house.

I love my pets, and they love me.
I love my pets. They're my family.
I don't have any brothers or sisters, you see.
My pets are my family!

I have a bird [ ] and a dog. [ ]
I have a rabbit [ ] and a frog. [ ]
All these animals live with me.
My pets are my family!

2 **Play a chain game.**

I have a bird.

I have a bird and a dog.

I have a bird and a dog and a frog.

3))) **Listen and say the chant.**

I have a hamster in my house.
A hungry hamster in my house.

Lesson 6

1))) Listen and read.

I Have a lot of Friends!

1

What's that, Libby?

It's an email from my sister. She's in Australia.

2

How many sisters do you have?

I have two sisters. Their names are Lisa and Laura.

3

LISA

Hi Libby,
How are you? I'm in Sydney. I love Australia. I have a big apartment, but I don't have a yard.
I have a car now, and two cats.
Write soon.
Love,
Lisa

4

Do you have any brothers or sisters, Ellie?

No, I don't.

But you have a lot of friends. Send them an email.

5

ELLIE

Hello friends,
Come and play today.
Love,
Ellie

Good idea!

6

See. You have a lot of friends.

Ooh. Yes, I do!

Ping! Ping! Ping!

2 Look at the picture below. Complete the blanks for Tom.

1 Do you have any _____ brothers, Tom?

2 _____.

3 Their _____ Jack and Bobby.

1))) **Listen and read.**

What Animals Need

Before

Do you have a house with a big yard?
Do you love animals?

Buddy is hungry. Please help.

Give Buddy a warm bed and a home.

After

Now I have a big yard to play in.

I have food and water.

I have a warm bed and a big family.
I love my family!

2 **Check (✔) the things that animals need.**

food	✔	a bike		a bed	
water		a home		a TV	

3 **Class survey. Ask and answer.**

Do you have any pets?

Yes, I do. I have a rabbit.

4 **Class Vote!**

Cats or dogs?

Find Out More!

Choose another animal. Find out what they need. Search the Internet or ask your teacher.

Project

Prepare

1 Make a funny family.

Showcase

2 Tell the story. Use your funny family.

I'm Nadia. I have a big family.

1))) **Listen and match.**

1

2

3

Jake ☐　　　Emily ☐　　　Brad ☐

2 **Look and complete the blanks.**

Boy: Do you have _____any_____ pets?

Girl: Yes, I _____. I have a _____
and a dog. Their _____ are Kitty
and Lucky. I _____ two hamsters.
_____ names _____ Harry and Henry.

 3 **Think about Chapter 6. Color the books.**

GREAT!

OK.

I'M NOT SURE.

Treasure Hunt!

Look back at pages
4 and 5. Find:

a rabbit

1)) Listen, read, and number. Then say.

TYRANNOSAURUS REX

1 a big head
2 a short neck
3 a big body
4 a long tail
5 two long legs
6 two big feet
7 two short arms
8 two small hands

Listen, read, and number.

My monster has three legs and a short tail. It has a long neck. ☐

My monster is brown. It has a big head and a small body. It has two long arms. ☐

My monster is small and black. It has four small hands. It doesn't have any legs. ☐

2 **Look at the other monster. Circle the correct description.**

1 It has a (big) / small head.

2 It has two / doesn't have any arms.

3 It has two / doesn't have any legs.

4 It has two / four hands.

Grammar Central

It **has a** big head.
It **has four** legs.
It **doesn't have any** arms.

Lesson 3

Tell Me a Story

1))) Listen and read. Then act out.

Story

4 OK Doodle, come with me. Where's your mom? Do you have a mom?

Mama! Mama!

No. I'm not your mom. My name's Jake.

Jakejakejake.

6 Eww! It's small and green. Look. It has long arms and short legs.

Ha, ha ha! Jake has a funny pet. It's ugly.

Ouch! My hand hurts.

The next day ...

8 Mama, Mama!

2 Look at the story and think. What's it about?

3)》 Listen and read. What does Doodle have?

short legs

big feet

long arms

Lesson 4

Time to Think

I Can Read!

When do we use these?

1 Read the story in your Reader.

2 Check (✔) Doodle's mom.

3 Who are your good friends?

My good friends are _____

4 Talk about the story.

Do you know another story about aliens?

Lesson 5

1))) **Listen and check (✔) the correct alien. Then sing.**

I'm an Alien

I have one big eye,
I don't have a nose,
I have three big ears,
And six little toes.

I have long green hair,
On my big head.
I have a small mouth,
My mouth is red.

I'm an alien. I'm a small, green alien.
I have one big eye on my face!
I'm an alien. I'm a small, green alien.
I come from Outer Space!

2 **Play a guessing game.**

How many eyes does it have?

It has six eyes. It doesn't have a mouth.

Number 3 is your alien!

3))) **Listen and say the chant.**

The moon has a face. A face in space.
That face in space is the moon.

Lesson 6

1))) **Listen and read.**

Biblio in Love!

1

What's the matter, Biblio?

I don't feel well. There's a new robot.

Don't worry. You're our favorite robot!

2

But this new robot is big and white. She has two blue eyes and a big mouth. She's ... beautiful!

3

How many legs does she have?

She doesn't have any legs. She has four black feet.

4

Where is she?

She's next to the elevator. Come and see!

5

Sigh!

Oh, Biblio! It's the copy machine! Are you in love?

2 **Complete the description of Biblio.**

1 He has _____two_____ eyes.

2 He _____ any ears.

3 He _____ any legs.

4 How many arms does he have?

_____

Grammar Central

She **has** two eyes.
How many legs **does she have**?
She **doesn't have** any legs.

1))) Listen and read. Then number.

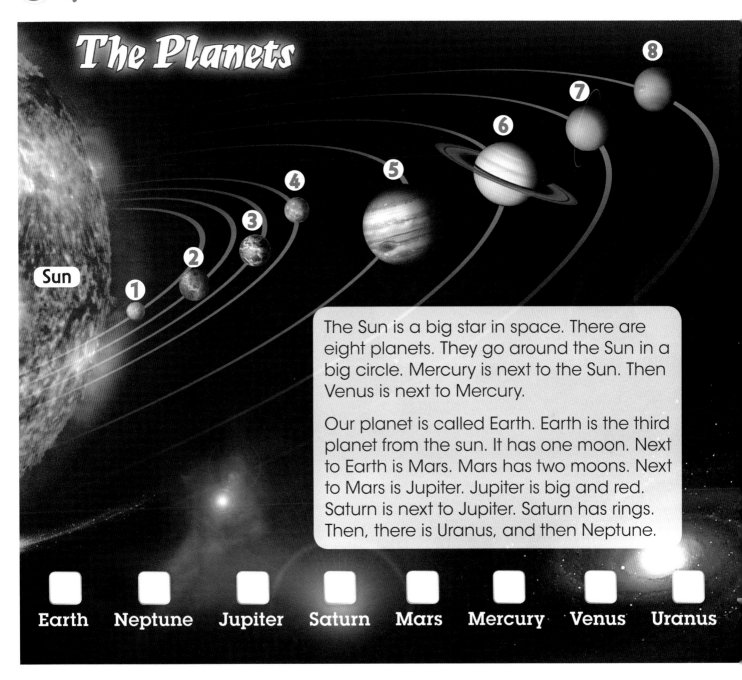

The Planets

Sun

The Sun is a big star in space. There are eight planets. They go around the Sun in a big circle. Mercury is next to the Sun. Then Venus is next to Mercury.

Our planet is called Earth. Earth is the third planet from the sun. It has one moon. Next to Earth is Mars. Mars has two moons. Next to Mars is Jupiter. Jupiter is big and red. Saturn is next to Jupiter. Saturn has rings. Then, there is Uranus, and then Neptune.

Earth   Neptune   Jupiter   Saturn   Mars   Mercury   Venus   Uranus

2 Class Vote!

Are there any aliens in space?
Yes or no?

Find Out More!
Find more facts about the planets.
Search the Internet or ask your teacher.

Project

Prepare

1 Make an alien.

Showcase

2 Tell the story. Use your aliens.

Look. It has long arms and short legs.

1))) Listen and check (✔) the correct monster.

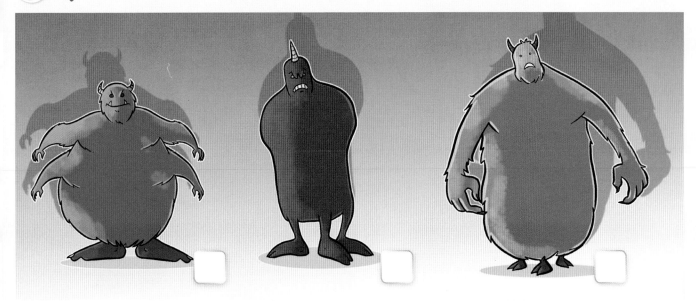

2 Write T (Tom) or B (Biblio).

1 He has two legs.   T
2 He has long arms.   B
3 He has two ears.
4 He doesn't have a nose.
5 He doesn't have any feet.

3 Think about Chapter 7. Color the books.

GREAT!

OK.

I'M NOT SURE.

Treasure Hunt!

Look back at pages 4 and 5. Find:

a long tail

I Like Food!

Lesson 1

💡 1))) Listen and number. Then say.

Menu

pizza

chicken

pasta

burger

fish

green beans

broccoli

peas

salad

fries

1 🔊 **Listen, read, and match.**

1

I like chicken and pasta. I like broccoli, but I don't like peas.

2

I like pizza, but I don't like pasta. I like salad.

3

I like burgers and fries. I like peas, but I don't like salad.

2 🔊 **Listen and check (✔) (I like …) or cross (✗) (I don't like …) for Ana.**

	salad	broccoli	chicken	fish	fries	peas	pasta	pizza
Ana	✔							
Me								

3 **Now complete the chart for you.**

4 **Talk to a friend.**

I like salad, but I don't like broccoli.

Grammar Central

I **like** pizza.
I **don't like** broccoli.
I **like** pizza, but I **don't like** broccoli.

1))) Listen and read. Then act out.

I like this book, Tom.

Hmm, sorry. I don't. I like this book.

Oh! Me, too!

I LIKE CAKE

It's Monday. It's lunchtime.
"Do you have any cake?" asks Chip.

1

"Hmm. Pizza, please," says Chip.
"I like pizza, but I don't like salad.
I don't like anything green."

3

"No, I don't," says Chef.
"Lunch today is chicken and green beans."

5

"No, I don't," says Chef.
"Lunch today is pizza and salad."

2

It's Tuesday. It's lunchtime.
"Do you have any cake?"
asks Chip.

4

"Hmm. Chicken, please," says Chip.
"I like chicken, but I don't like green beans. I don't like anything green."

6

2 Look at the story and think. Where are they?

3))) Listen and read. What food is in the story?

pizza

fish

salad

Lesson 4

Time to Think

1))) Read the story in your Reader.

I Can Read!
What are these?
"   "

2 Why is Chip unhappy?

....

3 Draw food that makes you happy.

4 Talk about the story.

Do you know another story about food?

  ))) **Listen and match. Then sing.**

Ice Cream and Cake

On Monday, I have salad.
On Tuesday, I have cheese.
On Wednesday, I have chicken.
More chicken, please!

On Thursday, I have pasta.
On Friday, I have rice.
Saturday, is pizza night.
Mmm! Pizza's very nice!

Sunday, is my favorite day.
You'll love the food I make!
For a special treat,
I have ice cream and cake!

2 **Write about your food. Then talk with a friend.**

On Monday I have pizza.

3))) **Listen and say the chant.**

Chicken and cheese, chicken and cheese,
More chicken and cheese, but no fish, please!

Lesson 6

1))) **Listen and read.**

Menu Mix-Up!

1. Hmm. I like chicken, but I don't like pizza. Do you like pizza?

Yes, I do.

LUNCH MENU
Pizza / Chicken
Salad / Rice
Cake / Ice cream

2. Chicken and rice, please, Biblio.

Pizza and salad, please.

LUNCH MENU
Pizza / Chicken
Salad / Rice
Cake / Ice cream

OK.

3. LUNCH MENU
Pizza / Chicken
Salad / Rice
Cake / Ice cream

Do you like cake, Tom?

Yes, I do.

Me, too. Two pieces of cake, please.

4. Uh ... OK. Ice cream?

Yes, please.

5. Oh!

Here you are!

LUNCH MENU
Pizza / Chicken
Salad / Rice
Cake / Ice cream

I don't like pizza with ice cream!

2 **Complete the blanks for Ellie.**

1 Do you like _____ pizza?

2 _____.

3 _____ chicken?

4 _____.

Grammar Central

Do you like pizza?
Yes, I do. / No, I don't

1))) **Listen and read.**

Lunchtime

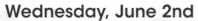

Tuesday, June 1st
This is my lunch today. There's cheese pizza with salad. Pizza is ok, but not every day. I like salad. It's good for you. There's ice cream, too. I like ice cream, but it's not very healthy!

Wednesday, June 2nd
Ugh! A terrible lunch today. Burger and fries. No vegetables! I don't like burgers and fries. They aren't healthy.

Thursday, June 3rd
Lunch today is chicken, rice, broccoli, and fruit. Very healthy! I like rice, and I love chicken. Fruit is OK.

What do you think? Which lunch do you like? What do you have for lunch? Show me your pictures!

2 **Write the food words in the correct places.**

Healthy food   Unhealthy food

salad

3 **Class Vote!**

Ice cream or fruit?

Find Out More! ↖
Find three more healthy foods.
Search the Internet or ask your teacher.

Lesson 8

Prepare

1 Make different food.

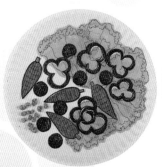

Showcase

2 Tell the story. Use your food.

Lunch today is pizza and salad.

1)) **Listen and check (✔) (I like...) or cross (✗) (I don't like...).**

 ✔

2 **Write answers for you.**

1 Do you like cake? ....

2 Do you like cheese? ....

3 Do you like ice cream? ....

4 Do you like fish? ....

5 Do you like rice? ....

3 **Think about Chapter 8. Color the books.**

GREAT!

OK.

I'M NOT SURE.

Treasure Hunt!

Look back at pages 4 and 5. Find:

Monday

))) Listen and number. Then say.

Get in Shape!

ride a bike ☐

run ☐ 1 ☐

swim ☐

dance ☐

skate ☐

play soccer ☐

1

2

3

4

5

6

Fitness is Fun

1))) **Look, listen, and (circle).**

1 It (can) / can't swim.   3 It can / can't ride a bike.

2 It can / can't run.   4 It can / can't skate.

2))) **Listen and check (✔) (Yes, I can.) or cross (✗) (No, I can't.) for Uma and Fred.**

Can you ...	Uma	Fred	Me
ride a bike?	✔		
swim?			
play soccer?			
dance?			
skate?			
run?			

3 Now complete the chart for you.

4 Talk to a friend.

> I can run, but I can't swim.

Grammar Central

He **can** run.
He **can't** skate.
Can you ride a bike?
Yes, **I can.**/No, **I can't.**

1 Listen and read. Then act out.

The Magic Violin

Look at this violin, Ellie. It's magic.

Don't be silly, Libby!

THE MAGIC VIOLIN

It's true. Listen to this story.

1 In our town,
There's a man named Tim.
He can't drive a cart,
But he can play the violin.

3 Look at those fish.
Those fish can fly!

4 Fish can't fly.
Don't be silly, Tim.

2 He can sing and dance,
This man named Tim,
And strange things happen,
When he plays his violin.

5 Oh, yes, they can,
When I play my violin.

2 Look at the story and think. What's it about?

3 Listen and read. What things are in the story?

fish ☐

cat ☐

violin ☐

I Can Read!

Is this story better
read out loud?
Which words rhyme?

1)) **Read the story in
your Reader.**

2 **Check (✔) what the fish can do in the story.**

fly ☐   sing ☐   dance ☐

3 **Write another verse. Then draw.**

Look at those ....

Those .... can ....!

.... can't ....

Don't be silly, Tim.

Oh, yes, they can,

When I play my violin.

4 **Talk about the story.**

Do you know
another rhyming
story?

Lesson 5

   Listen and number. Then sing.

Let's Play Together

Can you play the piano, piano, piano? ☐ 2
Can you play the piano?
Yes, I can.

Can you play the drums, drums, drums? ☐
Can you play the drums?
Yes, I can.

Can you play the guitar …? ☐

Can you play the tambourine …? ☐

Can you play the recorder …? ☐

Can you play the violin …? ☐

Let's all play together, together, together
Let's all play together.
Yes, we can!

2 Ask and answer.

Can you play
the piano?

No, I can't.

3 Listen and say the chant.

Bang! Bang! Bang! Drum. Drum. Drum.
Bang, bang, bang on the drum, drum, drum!

Lesson 6

1))) **Listen and read.**

Story Central Has Talent!

Look. There's a Talent Show on Friday. Can you play the piano, Ellie?

No, I can't play the piano, but I can sing.

Can Tom play the piano?

No, he can't, but he can play the guitar.

Yes, I can play the guitar, but I can't sing.

Wow! They're fantastic.

Now we have Biblio!

Wow! He can sing and he can dance.

He can play the guitar and he can skate. Ha ha!

But he can't stop!

And the winner is … Biblio!

Hooray!

2 **Complete the blanks for Tom and Ellie.**

1 Tom can _play the guitar_.

2 He can't _____.

3 _____ he sing? _____.

4 Ellie _____ sing.

5 She _____ play the piano.

Grammar Central

Can she sing?
Yes, she can. /
No, she can't.

Chapter 9

94

1))) **Listen and read.**

World Instruments

This instrument is from Australia. It's a **didgeridoo**. It's very long. It comes from a tree. You play the didgeridoo with your mouth. Native Australian people sing and dance to the sound of the didgeridoo.

This instrument is from Tibet. It's a **Tibetan hand bell**. It's very small. Tibetan hand bells can be used in meditation. People in Tibet play the hand bell with their left hand.

This instrument is from Hawaii. You play it with your nose! It's called a **Hawaiian nose flute**. It's long and thin.

Can you play any musical instruments? Do you use your mouth, hands, or nose?

2 (Circle) **T (true) or F (false).**

1 The didgeridoo is from Australia.   (T)/ F
2 You play the didgeridoo with your nose.   T / F
3 The Tibetan hand bell is very small.   T / F
4 You play the Tibetan hand bell with your right hand.   T / F
5 The Hawaiian nose flute is from Europe.   T / F

3 **Class Vote!**

Play or listen to music?

Find Out More! ↖

Find out about another unusual instrument from around the world. What parts of the body do you use to play it?

Prepare

1 Make an instrument.

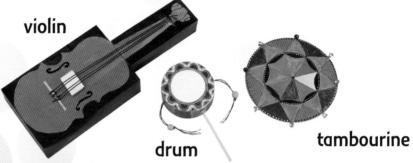

violin

drum

tambourine

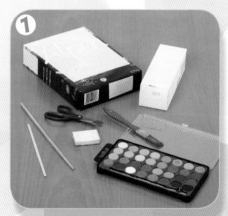

Showcase

2 Tell the story. Use your instruments.

Birds can't dance.
Don't be silly, Tim.

Oh, yes, they can,
When I play my violin.

1))) **Listen and check (✔) (Yes, he can.) or cross (✗) (No, he can't.). Then write answers.**

swim ✔   skate ☐   ride a bike ☐

dance ☐   play soccer ☐

1 Can he swim? _Yes, he can._
2 Can he ride a bike? _____
3 Can he skate? _____
4 Can he dance? _____
5 Can he play soccer? _____

2 **Write answers for you.**

1 Can you skate? _____
2 Can you play the guitar? _____
3 Can you ride a bike? _____
4 Can you swim? _____

3 **Think about Chapter 9. Color the books.**

GREAT!

OK.

I'M NOT SURE.

Treasure Hunt!

Look back at pages 4 and 5. Find:

skates

Grammar Reference

Chapter 1 Grammar

What is it? **It's a** pencil.
It isn't a pen.
Is it an eraser? Yes, **it is.** / No, **it isn't.**

What color is it?
It's red.
An orange notebook.

Sentence Maker: **How many sentences can you make?**

It's	a	red	pen.
		yellow	pencil.
		blue	eraser.
		green	notebook.
		brown	book.
It isn't	an	orange	ruler.

Think Again!

it's = it is
it isn't = it is not

Think Again!

a crayon / **an** eraser
a black notebook / **an orange** ruler
~~a book red~~

Chapter 2 Grammar

This is **my** robot. **That**'s **my** bike.
Is **this your** teddy bear? Is **that your** car?
Yes, **it is.** / No, **it isn't.**

How old are you?
I'm six.
How old is he/she?
He's/She's seven.

When's your/his/her birthday?
It's in June.

Think Again!

✔ Yes, **it is.**
✘ ~~Yes, **it's.**~~

Sentence Maker: How many sentences can you make?

Is	this	my	car?
		your	teddy bear?
	that	his	bag?
		her	doll?
			bike?

Chapter 3 Grammar

What are these? What are those?
They're lions/monkeys/giraffes.

They're hungry.
They aren't scary.

I'm tall.

Are crocodiles scary?
Yes, **they are**. / No, **they aren't**.

Think Again!
one tiger, one elephant
two tigers, five elephants

Think Again!
they**'re** = they **are**
they **aren't** = they **are not**

Sentence Maker: How many sentences can you make?

These	lions	are	scary.	They	aren't	scary.
Those	tigers		big.			big.
	elephants		hungry.			hungry.
	crocodiles		small.			small.
	giraffes		tall.			tall.
	monkeys		thin.			thin.

Grammar Reference
Chapter 4 Grammar

Where's the book?
It's **in** the living room.
It's **in/on/under/behind** the table.

Sit down. / Come in.
Don't sit down. / **Don't** come in.

Sentence Maker: How many sentences can you make?

The	cat	is	in	the	bag.
	pen	isn't	on		desk.
	bag		under		bed.
	crayon		behind		closet.
	pencil				bedroom.
	book				kitchen.

Chapter 5 Grammar

There's a hospital. **There are** four malls.

Is there a hospital?

Yes, **there is**. / No, **there isn't**.

How many malls **are there**?
There's one mall.
There are two malls.

Go straight.
Take the first/second/third left/right.
It's **next to** / **across from** the park.

Sentence Maker: How many sentences can you make?

There's	a	hospital.
		library.
There isn't		park.
There are	two	malls.
	three	movie theaters.
	four	cafés.
	five	
	six	

Chapter 6 Grammar

I have a brother / three brother**s**.
I don't have a grandpa.

Do you have any brothers or sisters?
Yes, **I do. I have** two brothers.
No, **I don't. I don't have any** brothers or sisters.

How many aunts and uncles **do you have**?
I have two aunts. **Their** names are Sally and Jess.

Think Again!

I have a brother
and a sister.
I don't have any
brothers **or** sisters.

Think Again!

They're my brothers.
Their names are Gary
and Jake.

Sentence Maker: How many sentences can you make?

I	have	a/an	mom.
		one	dad.
		two	brother(s).
		three	sister(s).
		four	grandma(s).
		five	grandpa(s).
	don't have	any	aunt(s).
			uncle(s).

Grammar Reference
Chapter 7 Grammar

It has a small head / **four** legs.
It doesn't have a big head.
It doesn't have any arms.

He/She has blue eyes.
He/She doesn't have long hair.

Does he/she/it have long legs?
Yes, **he/she/it does.** / No, **he/she/it doesn't.**

How many legs **does it have**?
It has two.

Think Again!

I don't have long hair.
It doesn't have long hair.

Think Again!

Does **it have** legs?
✔ Yes, **it does.**
✗ Yes, it have.

Sentence Maker: How many sentences can you make?

He	has	two	arms.
She	doesn't have	four	legs.
		long	eyes.
		short	
		big	hair.
		small	feet.
		blue	hands.
		brown	

Chapter 8 Grammar

I like pizza.
I don't like peas.
I like chicken, but **I don't like** fish.

Do you like cheese?
Yes, **I do.** / No, **I don't.**

On Friday, I have fries.

Think Again!

I like chicken **and** I **like** salad.
I **like** chicken, **but** I **don't like** salad.

Think Again!

Do you like salad?
Yes, **I do**.
✗ Yes, I like.

Sentence Maker: How many sentences can you make?

I like	fish	but	I like	peas.
I don't like	pizza	and	I don't like	cheese.
	chicken			salad.
	pasta			broccoli.
	fries			green beans.

Chapter 9 Grammar

I **can** ride a bike. I **can't** play the violin.
He/She can swim. **He/She can't** skate.
It can swim. / **It can't** play soccer.

Can you play the guitar?
Yes, **I can**. / No, **I can't**.
Can he/she/it swim?
Yes, **he/she/it can**. / No, **he/she/it can't**.

Think Again!

Can you play the guitar?
✔ Yes, **I can**.
✗ ~~Yes, I play~~.

Sentence Maker: How many sentences can you make?

I	can	play the violin.
You	can't	swim.
He		skate.
She		play soccer.
We		ride a bike.
		dance.
		play the guitar.
		run.

Macmillan Education
4 Crinan Street
London N1 9XW
A division of Macmillan Publishers Limited

Companies and representatives throughout the world

ISBN 978-0-230-44541-3
Pack ISBN 978-0-230-45197-1

Text © Viv Lambert ELT Limited and Mo Choy Design Ltd 2015
Design and illustration © Macmillan Publishers Limited 2015

Designed by Wild Apple Design Ltd.
Illustrated by Aardvart pp69, 88b; Ilias Arahovitis (Beehive Illustration) p78; Valentina Belloni (MB Artists) pp90–91, 93; Robin Boyden (Pickled Ink) pp70–71, 72, 73; Paco Cavero (Sylvie Poggio Artist Agency) pp17, 27t, 47, 57, 67, 77t, 87, 97; Inna Chernyak (Plum Pudding) pp30–31, 32, 33t; Marcus Cutler (Sylvie Poggio Artist Agency) pp80–81, 82, 83; Anna Hancock (Beehive Illustration) pp11rm, 13b, 19, 21r, 23b, 25b, 29, 31r, 33b, 35m, 39t, 41r, 43b, 49, 51r, 53b, 59, 61r, 63b, 71r, 73b, 81r, 89, 91r, 93b; Ellie Jenkins (Advocate Art) pp60–61, 62, 63; Ayesha Lopez (Advocate Art) pp40–41, 42, 43; Louise Redshaw (Plum Pudding) pp20–21, 22, 23; Laszlo Veres (Beehive Illustration) pp8, 38, 48, 68; Steven Wood (Advocate Art) pp 4-104 (border design and main character artwork) 4–5, 6–7, 10, 14, 20l, 24, 27m, 30l, 34, 40l, 44, 50l, 54, 60l, 64, 70l, 74, 80l, 84, 90l, 94; Patricia Yuste (Advocate Art) pp10, 11, 12, 13.
Cover design by Wild Apple Design Ltd.
Cover artwork Steven Wood (Advocate Art)
Cover photographs by Paul Bricknell
Picture research by Sally Cole (Perseverance Works Ltd)

Author's acknowledgements
Thank you to everyone at Macmillan for their support and for allowing us to work in 'our way'. For patience and tolerance of late-night working, thank you to our families.

The authors and publishers would like to thank the following for permission to reproduce their photographs:
Alamy/Juniors Bildarchiv GmbH pp12(l), 65(tr), Alamy/Blickwinkle p28(crocodile), Alamy/D.Boag p28(4), Alamy/P.Bradforth p78(pasta), Alamy/C.Bradshaw p18(car), Alamy/O.Calero p28(6), Alamy/Eureka p28(elephant), Alamy/V.Fischer p78(pizza), Alamy/T.Gainey p15(owl), Alamy/D.Hoare p85(fruit), Alamy/Imagebroker p88(bike), Alamy/N&M Jansen p85(burger), Alamy/T.King p18(d), Alamy/Kpzfoto p95(flag), Alamy/E.Lai p15(notebook), Alamy/D.Lee p85(chicken), Alamy/I.MacGregor p78(chicken), Alamy/LMiller p12(r), Alamy/Mylife Photos p88(swim), Alamy/Nordic Images p18(e), Alamy/M.Phillips p88(run), Alamy/Photocuisine p78(fish), Alamy/Golden Pixells LLc p88(dance), Alamy/Radius Images p28(2), Alamy/E.Remsberg p95(r), Alamy/R.Chapple Stock p79(3), Alamy/Travel South Africa p28(5), Alamy/A.Twort p78(beans), Alamy/Vanilla Echoes p78(salad), Alamy/Veterinary Images p65(tl), Alamy/Wacpan p15(pencil), Alamy/Life on White pp28(giraffe), 28(lion), 28(tiger); **Brand X** p85(pizza); **Corbis**/Cardinal p28(1), Corbis/Design Pics p35(zebras), Corbis/S.Frink p37(2), Corbis/W.Kaehler p28, Corbis/B.Kohlhas p15(tree), Corbis/P.McDonough p25(square), Corbis/Minden Pictures p37(4), Corbis/W. Wisniewski p28(3); **Digital Vision** p25(circle); **FLPA**/F.Lanting p35(giraffes), FLPA/Minden Pictures p37(1); **Getty Images**/Blend Images p79(2), Getty Images/Glow Décor p12(m), Getty Images/G.Doyle p58(tr), Getty Images/H.Dressler p95(l), Getty Images/Robert Harding World Imagery p35(lions), Getty Images/Imagebank p88(skate), Getty Images/istock Vectors p95(flags), Getty Images/Photographers Choice p53, Getty Images/Lonely Planet p55(3), Getty Images/Stockbyte p15(table), Getty Images/Vetta p79(1); **Getty RF** pp15(apple), 28(monkey), 78(broccoli), 85(ice cream); Image Source p78(fries); **Macmillan Australia** p25(rectangle); **Macmillan Publishers Limited**/P.Bricknell pp18(b), 18(f), Macmillan Publishers Limited/L.Payne p78(peas); **Photodisc** p85(salad); **Photoshot** p35(leopard), Photoshot/Imagebrokers p37(3); **Science Photo Library**/NASA/JPL p75; **Stockbyte** p25(triangle); **Superstock**/Age fotostock p95(c), Superstock/Blend Images pp58(c), 88(soccer), Superstock/Design Pics p45(m), Superstock/Imagebroker.net p53(2), Superstock/Loop Images p45(t); **Thinkstock**/Henera Technologies p13; **Up The Resolution** p78(burger).
Prop arwork by Carla Dury
Commissioned photography by MM Studios pp9, 16, 19, 26, 36, 39, 46, 56, 65, 66, 76, 86, 96.

Printed and bound in Thailand

2020 2019 2018 2017
11 10 9 8 7 6 5